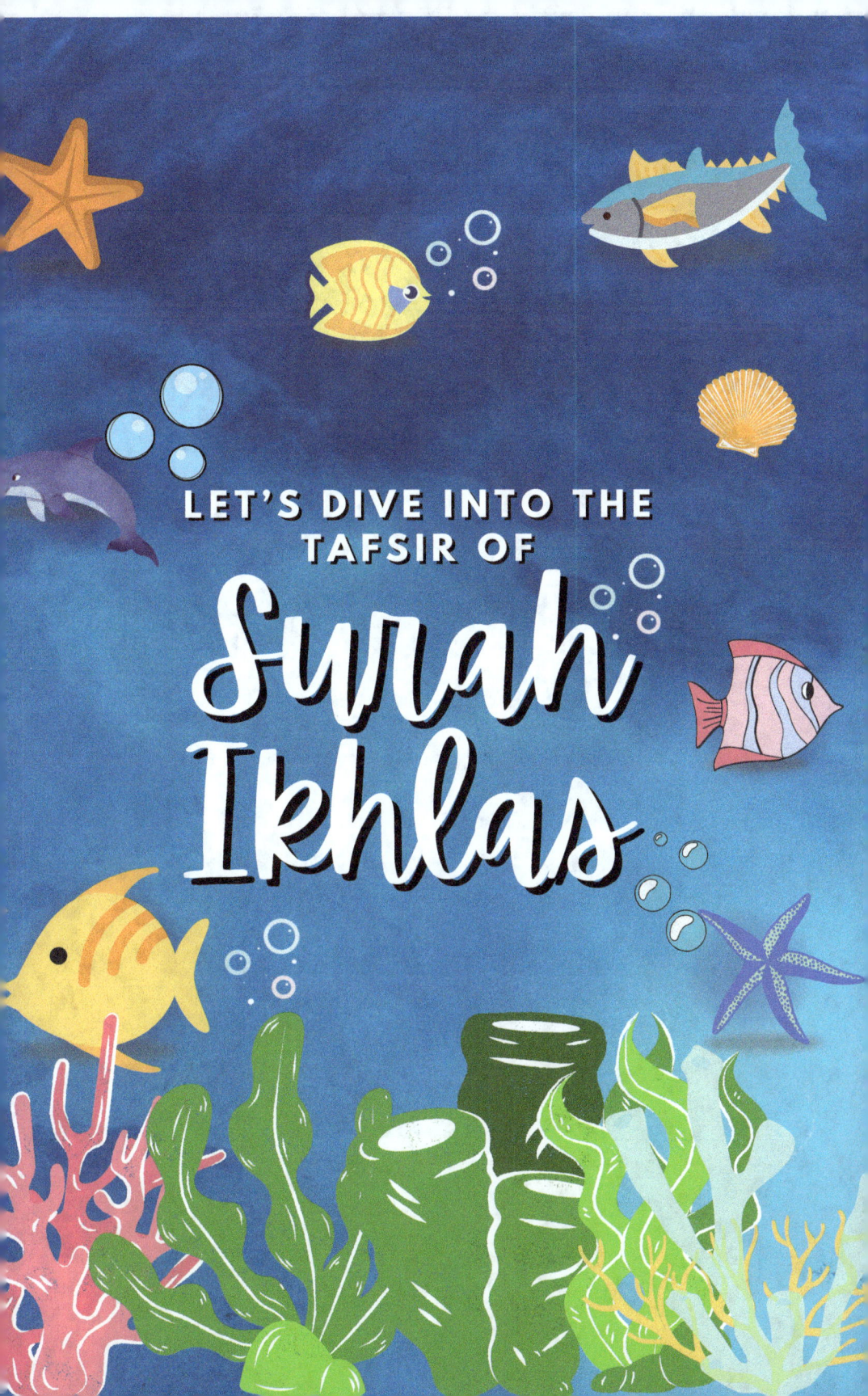

FIRST, LET'S RECITE THE SURAH TOGETHER!

بِسْمِ ٱللَّهِ ٱلرَّحْمَٰنِ ٱلرَّحِيمِ 1

قُلْ هُوَ ٱللَّهُ أَحَدٌ 2

ٱللَّهُ ٱلصَّمَدُ 3

لَمْ يَلِدْ وَلَمْ يُولَدْ 4

وَلَمْ يَكُن لَّهُۥ كُفُوًا أَحَدٌۢ 5

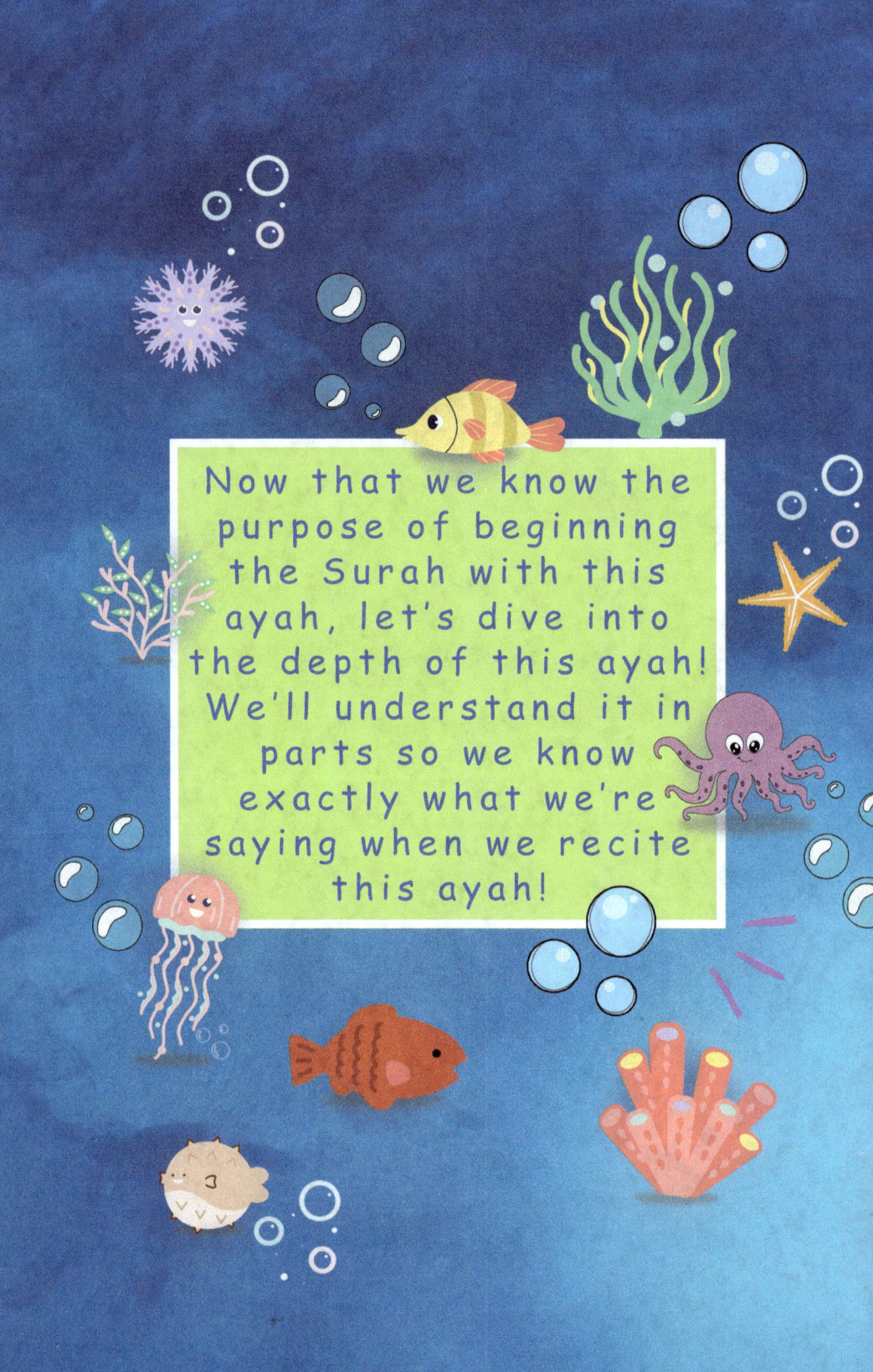

Now that we know the purpose of beginning the Surah with this ayah, let's dive into the depth of this ayah! We'll understand it in parts so we know exactly what we're saying when we recite this ayah!

ب

means with! Now, let's look a little deeper. The 'with' over here means with the help of! For example, we say I wrote with my pencil, I drew with my colours, I cut with the scissors. That means, I did the work with the help of that thing! The same way, here, we are saying "with the help of".

ٱلرَّحْمَٰنِ ٱلرَّحِيمِ

are the names of Allah that He chose to use in this ayah! Allah has 99 names and out of all of them, He chose these two to introduce Himself at the beginning of the glorious Quran, and this Surah too! He chose His names of mercy, that means He wants to be known by His mercy! Ar-Rahman and Ar-Raheem, both, have to do with Allah's mercy.

Therefore, when we say
بِسْمِ ٱللَّهِ ٱلرَّحْمَٰنِ ٱلرَّحِيمِ
we are saying,
"I begin with the help of the name of Allah, the Most Beneficent, the Most Merciful!" We are asking Allah for His help and his mercy!

Can you spot a name of Allah in this ayah? Read it once again and look for it! Yes! It's Al Ahad! Let's dive into this ayah and understand the depth of it!

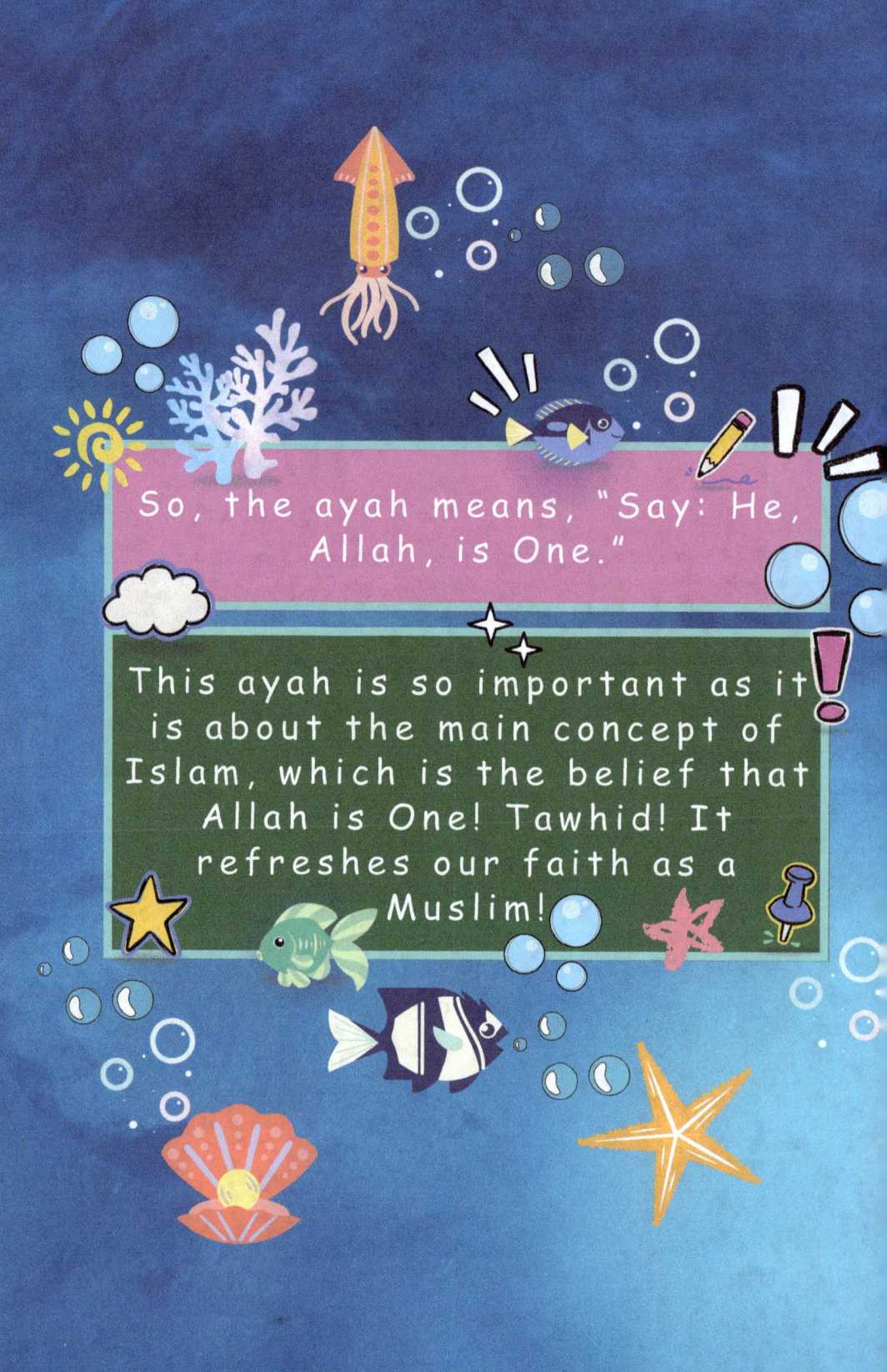

So, the ayah means, "Say: He, Allah, is One."

This ayah is so important as it is about the main concept of Islam, which is the belief that Allah is One! Tawhid! It refreshes our faith as a Muslim!

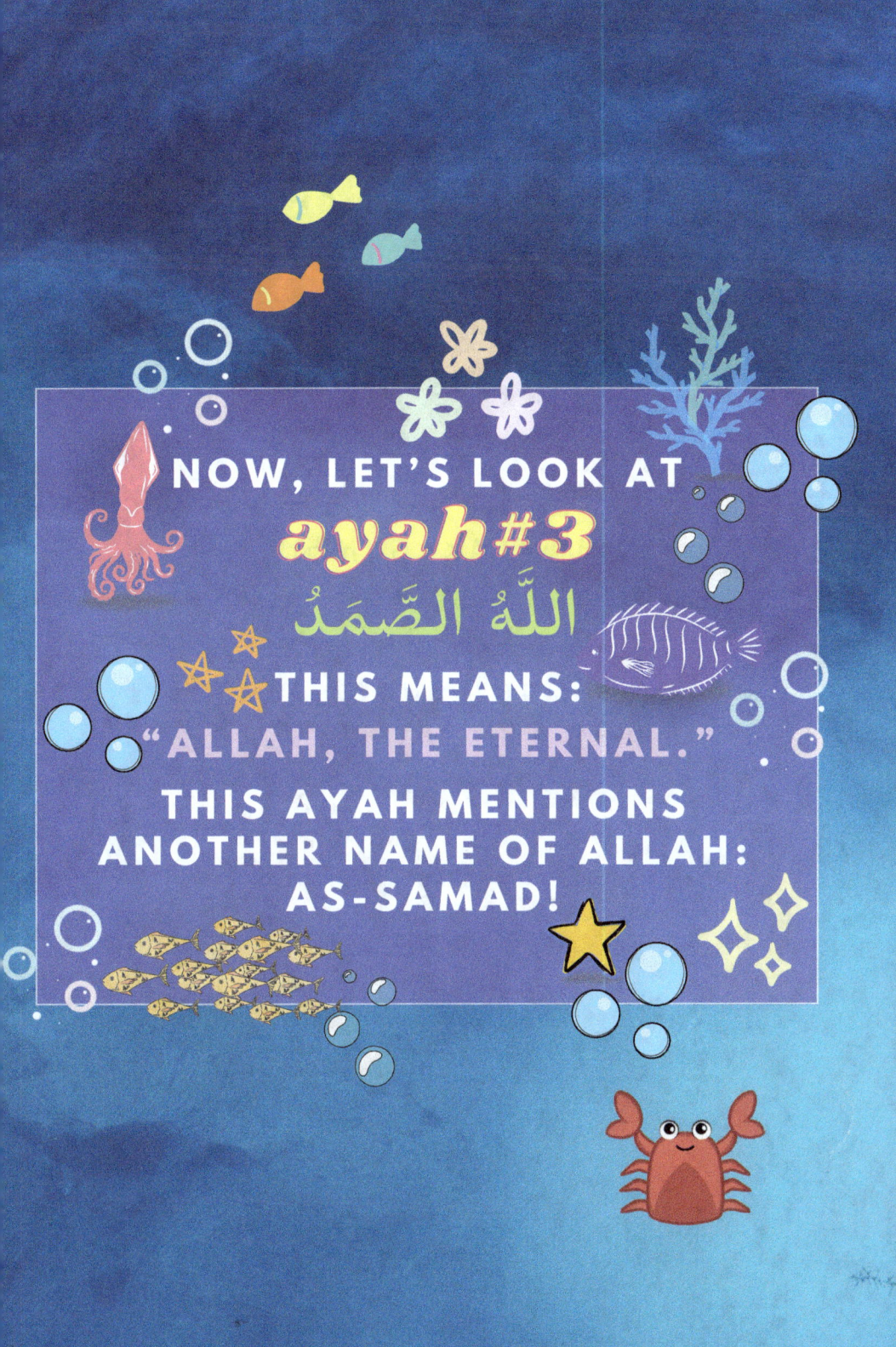

This ayah tells us that Allah is As-Samad. But what does that mean? Let's dive deeper and see what our beloved Imam Hussain (as) has told us about the meaning of Allah's name, As-Samad!

IMAM HUSSAIN (AS) HAS GIVEN US FIVE MEANINGS OF ALLAH'S NAME AS-SAMAD.

① As-Samad means the One whose Lordship is as much as it can possibly be! That means, Allah is the One who has the most authority, the ultimate power! He has control over everything, everything is under Him!

② As-Samad means the Everlasting! That means, Allah is the One who existed before everything else, and the One who will exist after everything else perishes. He is the only One who will last forever!

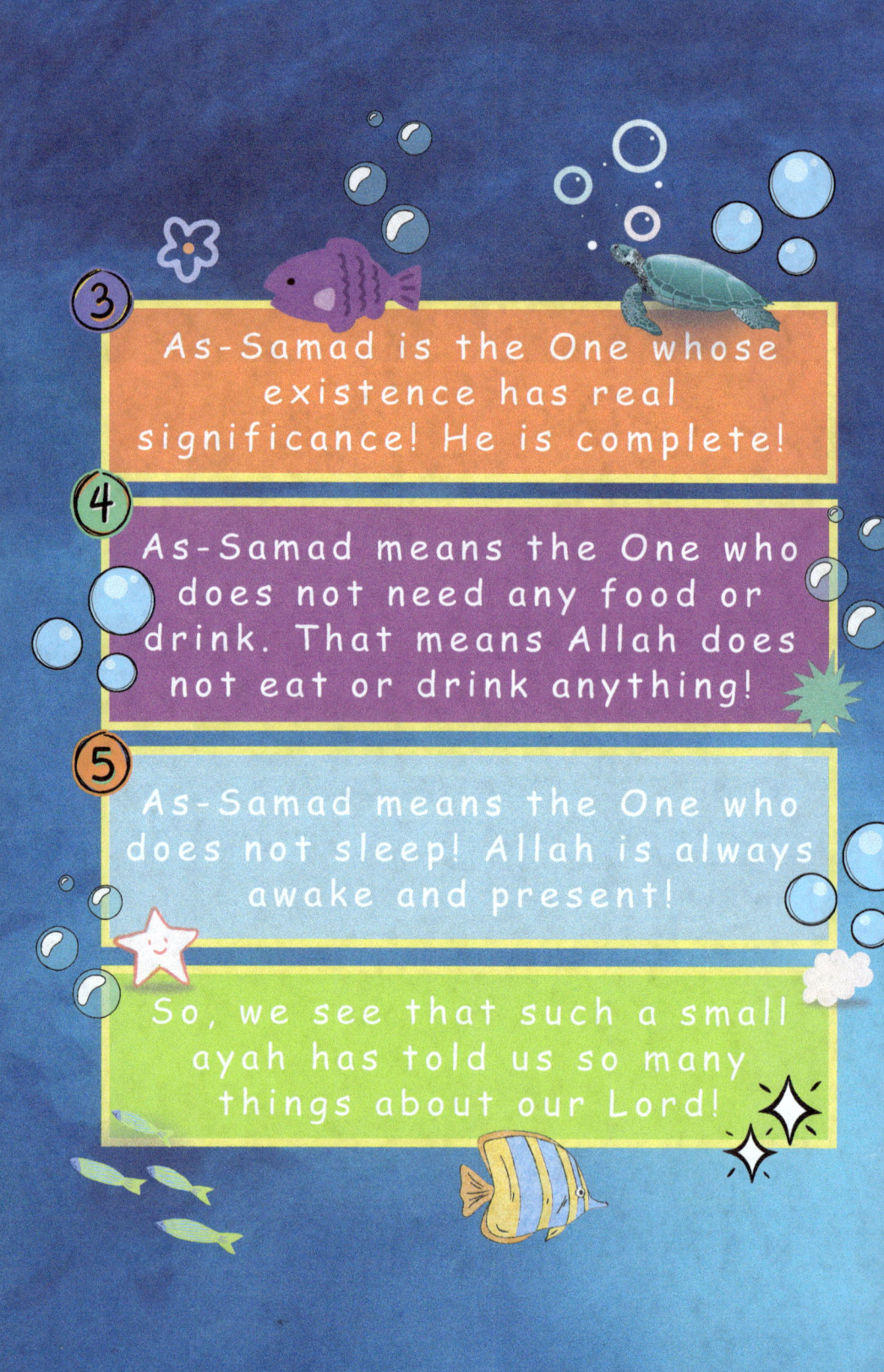

③ As-Samad is the One whose existence has real significance! He is complete!

④ As-Samad means the One who does not need any food or drink. That means Allah does not eat or drink anything!

⑤ As-Samad means the One who does not sleep! Allah is always awake and present!

So, we see that such a small ayah has told us so many things about our Lord!

This ayah brings light to another very core belief of ours as Muslims, and this belief is what makes us different from other religions such as Christianity!

This ayah tells us that Allah is not the son or child of anyone, and nor does He have any son or child. This ayah firmly rejects the belief of the Christians who claim that Jesus (Prophet Isa) is the son of God!

Similarly, there were people who claimed that angels are the daughters of Allah, but once again, this ayah clearly tells us that there is no such thing! And therefore, we must stay away from any such assumptions or false beliefs!

This ayah further speaks about our belief in Tawhid, the Oneness of Allah and the fact that no association can be made to Him!

This ayah concludes the Surah by giving us a summary of the entire Surah! Let's dive deeper and have a look at how beautifully this ayah ties up the Surah!

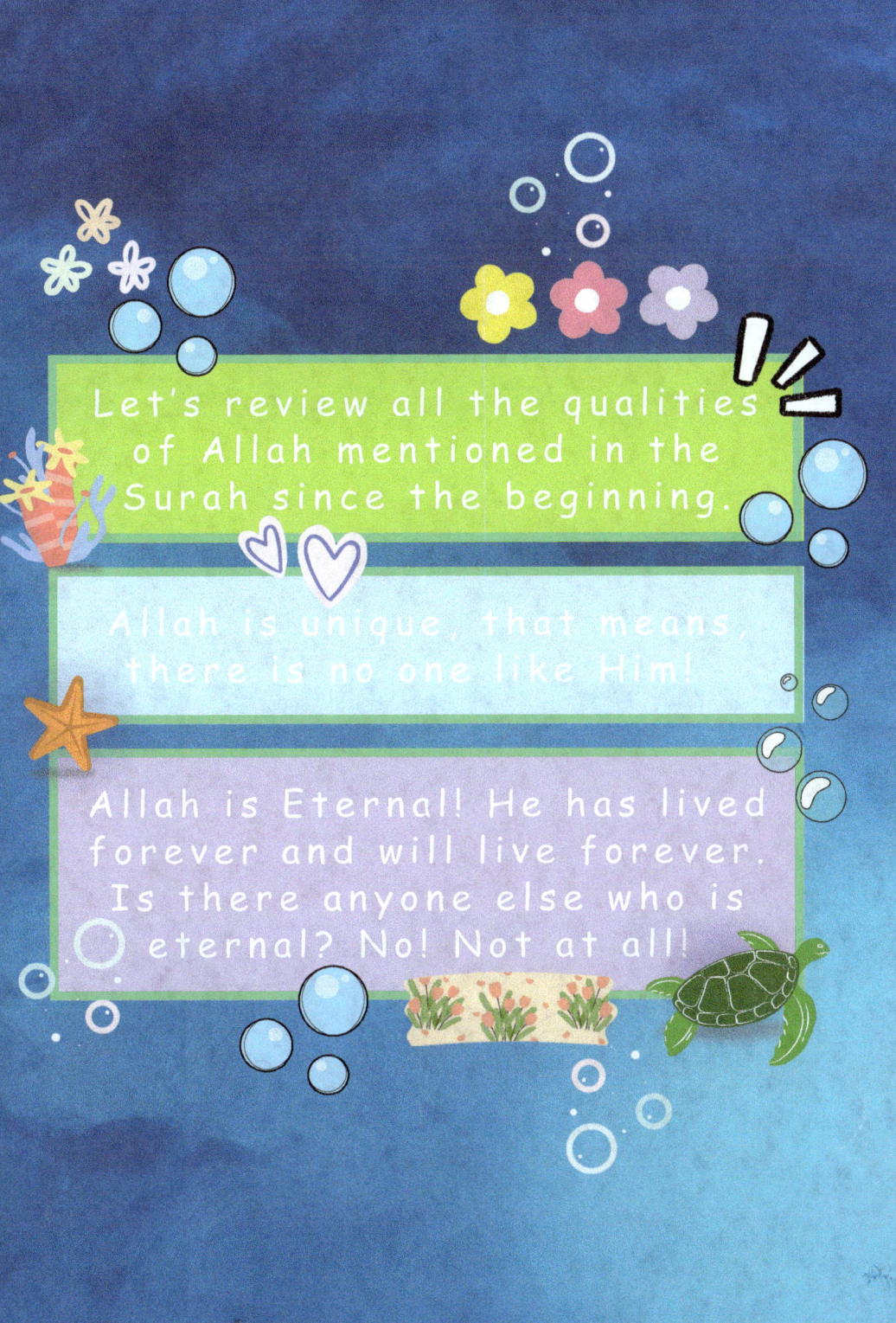

Allah has ultimate power! Is there anyone else who has this ultimate power? No! Not at all!

Allah doesn't need anything, not even food or drink! Is there anyone else who does not need anything? No! Not at all!

Allah does not sleep! Is there anyone else who does not sleep? No! Not at all!

And so, we come to the conclusion that the last ayah confirms, that there is no one like Allah!

www.ingramcontent.com/pod-product-compliance
Lightning Source LLC
Chambersburg PA
CBHW072003060526
44107CB00150B/388